MAY 1 2 2006

D1737593

Discovering
Cultures

Germany

Sharon Gordon

BENCHMARK BOOKS

MARSHALL CAVENDISH
NEW YORK

PUBLIC LIBRARY SAN MATEO, CALIFORNIA

Marshall Cavendish
99 White Plains Road
Tarrytown, New York 10591-9001
www.marshallcavendish.com

Text copyright © 2005 by Marshall Cavendish Corporation
Map and illustrations copyright © 2005 by Marshall Cavendish Corporation

All rights reserved. No part of this book may be reproduced or utilized in any form or by any means electronic or mechanical, including photocopying, recording, or by any information storage and retrieval system, without written permission from the copyright holders.

All Internet sites were available and accurate when sent to press.

Library of Congress Cataloging-in-Publication Data

Gordon, Sharon.
Germany / by Sharon Gordon.
p. cm. — (Discovering cultures)
Includes bibliographical references and index.
ISBN 0-7614-1792-3
1. Germany—Juvenile literature. I. Title. II. Series.
DD17.G67 2004
943—dc22   2004006132

Photo Research by Candlepants Incorporated
Cover Photo: Bryan F. Peterson/*Corbis*

The photographs in this book are used by permission and through the courtesy of; *SuperStock*: 11, Steve Vidler, 1, 32 (left); Hidekazu Nishibata, 16; Travel Pix Ltd., 33; *Corbis*: Premium Stock, 4, 20, 42 (right); Tibor Bognar, 6; Rob Schoenbaum 8; Richard Klume, 10, Archivo Icongraphico S.A., 14; Dallas & John Heaton, 15; Ediface, 17 (left); Bo Zaunders, 19; Owen Franken, 22, 23 (left); Andrew Cowin/Travel Inc., 24; John Gress/ Reuters, 26; Bettmann 27 (lower); Bob Krist, 29; Adan Woolfitt, 30, 31; Arnd Wiegmann/Reuters, 34; Bernard Bisson/SYGMA, 38; David Lees,44. *The Image Works*: Thomas Pflaum/VISUM, 7; Topham, 9, 43 (left); Francis Dean, 13 (right); David Frazier, 17 (right), 43 (lower right); Hermann Dornage/VISUM, 18; Sven Martson, 23 (right); Thomas Cojaniz/VISUM, 27 (top); Masakatsu Yamazaki, 32 (right); Shinichi Wakatsuki/HAGA, 35, 39. *Index Stock Imagery*: Stewart Cohen, 12; Zefa Visual Media, 36-37. *Photo Researchers Inc.*: William H. Mullins, 13 (left). *Envision*: Michael Howell, 28. *Getty Images*: 45; Taxi/Alexander Walters, back cover.

Cover: *Moritzburg Castle, Dresden, Germany*; Title page: *Bavarian boy in traditional dress*

Map and illustrations by Ian Warpole
Book design by Virginia Pope

Printed in China
1 3 5 6 4 2

Turn the Pages...

Where in the World Is Germany?

Germany is at the center of the European *continent*. It sits between the nations of eastern and western Europe. It is the third-largest nation in the European Union (EU) after France and Spain. It also has the most people of any country in the EU. It is a little smaller than the state of Montana.

Germany has nine neighbors. On the north, it shares a short border with Denmark. The North Sea and the Baltic Sea lie on either side of this coastline. Poland

The snowy peaks of the Bavarian Alps

Map of Germany

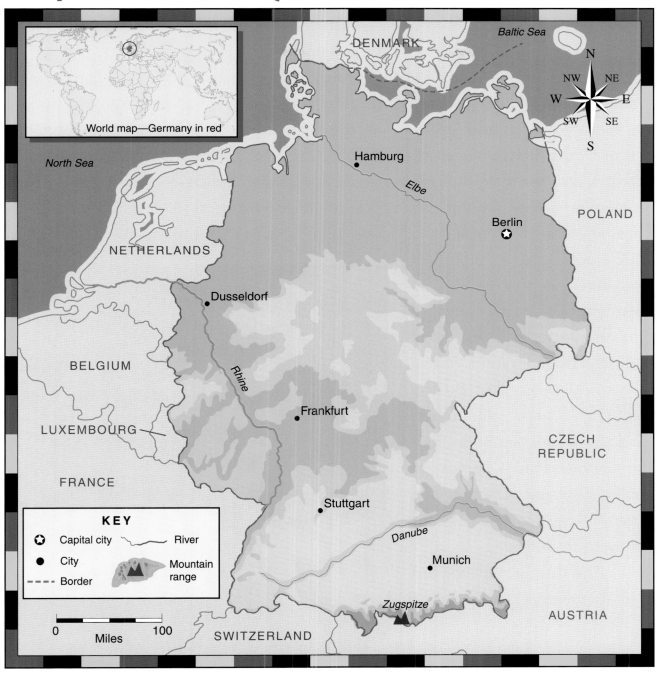

World map—Germany in red

DENMARK

Baltic Sea

North Sea

NETHERLANDS

BELGIUM

LUXEMBOURG

FRANCE

Hamburg

Elbe

Berlin

POLAND

Dusseldorf

Rhine

Frankfurt

CZECH
REPUBLIC

Stuttgart

Danube

Munich

Zugspitze

SWITZERLAND

AUSTRIA

KEY

✪ Capital city

● City

--- Border

River

Mountain range

0   Miles   100

N
NW   NE
W   E
SW   SE
S

and the Czech Republic are on the east. To the south are Austria and Switzerland. To the west are France, Luxembourg, Belgium, and the Netherlands.

In northern Germany, the land changes from place to place. The flat lowlands between the two northern seas are called the North German Plain. Most of the soil in this area is rich and fertile. There are many farms here. Hamburg is Germany's largest port. It has many canals that are used for transportation. The northwest coastal land has rocky soil and wide-open areas that are covered with shrubs, such as purple *heather*. On the coasts there are important ports for shipping, and lovely beaches. In the northeast is the Mecklenburg Lake District, which includes more than 1,000 lakes.

Berlin is the capital of Germany. For many years, it was an important center of industry. During World War II, almost 90 percent of Berlin's buildings were destroyed. Today, new buildings are going up and old buildings are being *restored*. Once again, many large companies are moving to Berlin.

The Central Uplands are in the middle of Germany.

A sculpture and modern buildings in Berlin

Dark evergreens in the Black Forest

This area has raised flatlands called plateaus. Deep river valleys cut through them. Small mountain ranges, such as the Harz Mountains, can also be found in central Germany. The beautiful Bavarian Forest is in east central Germany.

Southern Germany has many mountains and forests. The Black Forest in the southwest is named for its dark evergreen trees. The high snowy peaks of the German Bavarian Alps form the southern border with Austria and Switzerland. The tallest of these snowy peaks is Zugspitze, at 9,718 feet (2,962 meters). The Alps are popular with skiers and hikers. Tourists can stay at beautiful resorts. They can ride on cable cars that take them high into the mountains to see the views. Germany's largest lake, the Bodensee, is also in the south. It is called Lake Constance in English. Half of the Bodensee is in Germany, and the rest is in Switzerland and Austria.

Germany's coastal weather is different than that of the inland. The western parts of Germany are a little warmer and wetter than the rest of the country. The

A canal in Hamburg connects to the Elbe.

weather changes with the ocean currents and breezes. Southwest Germany gets a wind called the *sirocco*, which brings in warm air from the Mediterranean Sea.

Without the warming effects of the ocean, the climate of the eastern sections of Germany tends to be more extreme. Inland summers are hot and the winters are cold. Cologne in the west has an average of only forty-four frost days per year, but Berlin in the east has ninety.

Many of Germany's greatest cities grew up along important rivers. Trading towns like Hamburg, on the Elbe, and Frankfurt, on the Main, became centers of business. The Rhine is an important river that runs from Switzerland through Germany and into the Netherlands. It is 820 miles (1,319 kilometers) long and connects southern and northern Europe. The Rhine is always busy with cargo ships carrying goods between the nations and with tourists on sightseeing boats.

Lorelei Rock

At a steep turn in the Rhine River, near the town of Saint Goarshausen, there is a large slate rock called the Lorelei Rock. It rises almost 435 feet (132 m) above the water at the most narrow and deep part of the Rhine. Swirling water called *whirlpools* and rough rapids make it a dangerous place for ships. In the past, so many of them sank near the huge rock that a legend grew up around it. The legend says a beautiful young maiden named Lorelei became so sad when her true love betrayed her that she threw herself down from the rock into the water. After her death, her voice became a beautiful song, which called to passing sailors. When they looked up to see her, they took their eyes off the river and crashed their boats on the rocks.

What Makes Germany German?

A fountain in an old, historic town

Germany is rich in beauty and history. It is filled with small villages, charming towns, and old cities. German culture is thousands of years old. The Germanic tribes settled the land around 300 B.C.

Germany has many different regions, such as Bavaria or Prussia. Each region has its own traditions that are handed down through families. Often, Germans feel stronger ties to their region than to their nation.

German culture has helped shape the modern world. Some of the finest writers, composers, scientists, and thinkers have been Germans. Sigmund Freud was a pioneer in the area of psychology, the study of how people behave. Albert Einstein was a famous scientist who received the Nobel Prize in physics in 1921. Wolfgang Amadeus Mozart was one of the greatest composers who ever lived. He began his musical career at the age of four. Johannes Kepler was a German astronomer who studied the movement of the planets.

A famous German inventor named Johannes Gutenberg changed the world of books. Around 1450, Gutenberg invented movable type, which were tiny letters made of metal. The movable type was locked into a metal frame and covered with ink. Then paper was pressed onto it, creating a printed page. The machine that held the movable type and paper became known as a *printing press*. With the printing press, many copies of books could be made quickly. Within years, people around the world were able to own books. Gutenberg's first printing press can be seen in the Gutenberg Museum in Mainz.

A Bavarian man in traditional clothing

A memorial at the Dachau Concentration Camp

The world will never forget what happened in Germany during World War II. The Nazi Party was in charge of the government. It was led by a man named Adolf Hitler, who wanted to control the world and get rid of the Jews. He also hated other people who he felt were not as good as Germans. He built concentration camps where millions of men, women, and children were put to death by the Nazis.

Over the years, groups from different countries have come to live in Germany. Many people from Turkey came to Germany looking for work in the 1960s and 1970s. The Turks are the largest non-German group in the country. In fact, the most popular fast food today is the *doner kebab*, a Turkish meat sandwich.

The German shepherd is a breed of dog that is used for many important jobs. They were originally used to guard herds of sheep. These smart, strong dogs were used during World War I, and soldiers came home with stories of their courage in battle. They soon became very popular pets around the world. German shepherds have been trained to work with police. They also are taught to be Seeing Eye dogs for the blind.

German shepherd

The word *Volkswagen* means "people's car." The German Volkswagen was nicknamed "the Beetle" because its size and shape made it look like a bug. By 1972, the Volkswagen Beetle was the most popular car ever built. Today, there is a new version of the Volkswagen Beetle.

The German Volkswagen

Germany has given the world some fine musicians. Johann Sebastian Bach was known for his organ music. Many experts believe Ludwig van Beethoven wrote the greatest classical music of all time. At age twelve, he began to give piano lessons. He continued to write beautiful music even after he lost his hearing at a young age. Beethoven's "Ode to Joy" became the official song of the European Community in 1986. German composer Richard Wagner included German folklore in his grand operas.

Some of the most beloved children's stories came from the Brothers Grimm. *Grimms'*

Ludwig van Beethoven

Fairy Tales is a collection of old German folktales and poetry. Jakob and Wilhelm Grimm collected and published them in 1857. Eventually these folktales were sold around the world. They include Cinderella, Little Red Riding Hood, Sleeping Beauty, Snow White, and Hansel and Gretel.

Dirndl and Lederhosen

In the southern regions of Germany, both children and adults might wear *tracht*, or traditional clothing, during festivals or other special occasions. A German boy wears *lederhosen* (LAY-der-hoh-zen), which are short leather pants with suspenders. Lederhosen are worn with wool socks, heavy shoes, a white shirt, a vest and tie, and a felt cap with feathers to top it off. Young girls wear a *dirndl* (DERN-del), which is a dress with a full, colorful skirt. Sometimes a fancy lace blouse is worn underneath and an apron is worn over the skirt. A cap or hat may also be worn.

Living in Germany

Germany's official name is the Federal Republic of Germany. The country is divided into sixteen provinces, or states. They include Bavaria, Rhineland, and Lower Saxony. Each state can make its own laws, like those in the United States. However, they must also follow the guidelines of Germany's Basic Law, which is like the U.S. Constitution. This helps to make sure that all Germans have the same rights and living conditions.

About 80 percent of Germans live in cities or towns. Houses are expensive, so many people rent apartments. Most of these apartment buildings were built after WWII, since so many cities were bombed during the war. Cities that were not destroyed have narrow, twisting streets and charming old buildings. Gardens are popular, but are usually small. Sometimes, people own or rent a piece

Beautiful buildings line an old city street.

A crowded street in Cologne

Colorful balconies on an apartment building in Dusseldorf

of land near their apartment to grow summer fruits and vegetables.

Germans who live and work in the cities often use bicycles or public transportation to get around. Some cities have a downtown area called a "Fussganger zone." No cars or buses are allowed on the streets. People enjoy walking in these areas without any traffic.

Today, most Germans work in service industries, such as banking. Many people also work in factories making

Workers at the BMW factory in Munich

clothes or furniture. Germans make some of the best cars in the world. The famous BMW of Munich stands for "Bavarian Motor Works." Only a few Germans are farmers who grow crops such as fruit, grains, and potatoes. Vineyards along the Rhine and Mosel Rivers produce grapes for wines that are popular around the world.

Life in Germany's small villages and rural areas is slow and peaceful. There are winding streets and neat, old houses. Locals come to the town square to buy and sell products, and to talk with their neighbors. Villagers might earn a living making crafts, working on a farm, or commuting into a nearby city for factory and office jobs.

Vineyards in the countryside

In the Alps, there are sawmills that process trees used to make furniture and other products. Skiing is also an important business in the mountains. Many Germans work for hotels and restaurants at ski resorts.

Germans like to travel fast. Germany was one of the first countries to build highways, in 1913. These highways are called the *autobahn*. There are some autobahns where there is no speed limit. Some have up to ten lanes of cars. The Deutsche Bundesbahn and private companies have about 28,264 miles

Germany's express trains

(45,514 km) of train tracks within Germany. Their new intercity express trains speed between major cities at up to 150 miles (241 km) per hour!

Germans love to eat pork. The word "wurst" means sausage, and there are over 1,500 kinds of wursts in Germany. Each region of the country likes to make its sausage a little differently. The United States frankfurter, or "hot dog," came from a sausage made in Frankfurt. Braunschweiger, or liverwurst, is a spreadable sausage that comes from Braunschweig. Germans enjoy eating their pork sausages with pickled cabbage, sauerkraut, dumplings, or noodles.

Let's Eat!
German Potato Salad

Along with their wursts, Germans enjoy eating this tasty potato salad. It is a favorite at picnics and family celebrations.

Ingredients

12 medium potatoes

12 strips bacon

1 $1/2$ cups onion, chopped

$1/4$ cup all-purpose flour

$1/4$ cup sugar

1 tablespoon salt

1 teaspoon celery seed

1 teaspoon ground mustard

1 pinch pepper

1 $1/2$ cups water

$3/4$ cup vinegar

fresh parsley, chopped

In a saucepan, cook potatoes until just tender; drain. Peel and slice into a large bowl and set aside. In a skillet, cook bacon until crisp. Remove bacon and place on paper towels. Throw out all but 1/3 cup of bacon drippings. Saute onion in drippings until tender. Stir in the next six ingredients. Gradually stir in water and vinegar. Bring to a boil, stirring constantly. Cook and stir two minutes more. Pour over potatoes. Crumble bacon and gently stir into potatoes. Sprinkle with parsley. Makes twelve to fourteen servings.

School Days

The word *kindergarten* came from Germany. It means "child's garden." Kindergarten started in Germany in 1840 and is now popular in many countries around the world. German children do not have to attend kindergarten, but most of them do.

An elementary school student hard at work

All education in Germany is free, even the universities. Children learn math, science, literature, history, geography, music, and arts. In fifth grade they begin to learn a second language, usually English. In grades five to seven, they can learn other languages, such as French, Spanish, Latin, or Russian. German education encourages children to think clearly and become involved in class discussions.

The German school year starts between July and September. It ends between June and August. There is a six-week summer break. Every one of Germany's states has its own summer vacation time. The times are different from state to state so the beaches never get too crowded. German students have two weeks off in December and January and for Easter. They have another week off in the fall. In total, German children have 220 school days, compared with 180 in the United States.

A German teacher helps her student.

German students used to have to wear uniforms, but now they can wear everyday clothes. German children carry *schulranzen*, colorfully decorated square bags that are smaller than regular backpacks.

Schoolchildren start their day around 8:00 A.M. and are done by early afternoon. In the winter, it is quite dark when they go off to school in the morning. Students may walk, ride their bikes, or take a public bus. Many parents drive their children to school. In many of Germany's larger towns, there are bicycle paths that are separate from the roads and sidewalks. This makes them safe for traveling. Schoolchildren learn to watch for the special traffic lights on the bike paths.

After school, students have a hot meal called *mittagessen*, which is often the biggest meal of the day. German children try to use their afternoons to finish their homework, so they can have time for fun with their friends. They might go shopping, go to the movies, or play sports or board games. In some states, German children must also go to school on Saturday.

Going home at the end of the day

Elementary school, grades one to six, is called Grundschule. After graduating, a student can attend high school. A Gymnasium is a high school for students who will go to college. It goes through grade thirteen, one year more than U.S. high schools. Other students must choose between a Hauptschule (grades five through nine) and a Realschule. A Hauptschule is for students who want to learn a trade or get a job. The Realschule is for students who are not sure if they want to go to college or get a job instead. It prepares them for both. In recent years, Gesamtschulen schools, which offer all three choices in one school, have become more common.

Students in a Gymnasium often become "exchange students" in a different country during grade eleven. The most popular places to go are the United States and Britain. There are more than three hundred colleges and universities in Germany, most of which are free to German citizens.

All men must spend ten months in the military before the age of twenty-five. It is called National Service. They may serve in the army, navy, or air force. If they do not want to serve in the military, they can choose to do thirteen months of community service.

University buildings in Heidelberg

Schultute

German children look forward to their first day of school. That is because their parents or friends give them a big, colorful cardboard cone called a *schultute*. It helps children feel special on their first day of school. The schultute is filled with candy, nuts, and other treats. It also holds the student's school supplies, such as paper and pencils. It usually has a Fuller, or fountain pen, that sends ink right to the point of the pen. Most German children learn to write with a Fuller.

Just for Fun

Women's World Cup soccer

Soccer is Germany's favorite sport. It is called *fussbal* (football). German children, especially boys, join soccer clubs to play against other teams. In 2006, Germany will host the soccer World Cup. Germans also enjoy swimming. Most communities have a *schwimmbad*, or swimming pool, for the public to use. Sometimes, there is both an indoor and an outdoor pool.

German children also enjoy horseback riding, ice hockey, and volleyball. Beach volleyball is played in the summer. Windsurfing is becoming more popular, too. Sylt, an island in the North Sea, holds a World Cup in windsurfing each year.

Germans also love to play and to watch tennis. Germany has produced many fine tennis players who have won international titles. In 1988, Steffi Graf became the third woman in history to win a true grand slam by winning the Australian, French, U.S. Open, and Wimbledon singles

Time for a swim

titles. Boris Becker is a three-time Wimbledon champion, and one of the most outstanding tennis players in history.

Germany has many mineral springs that bubble up from the earth. Many people believe that the water from the springs can get rid of their aches and pains. Spas have been built around the springs so that people can come and bathe in the water. Germany has about 250 of these health spas, including Baden-Baden in the Black Forest. Some spas let people drink the mineral water for their health.

German adults and children are great readers. They like to spend their spare time with a good book. That is why the Frankfurt Book Fair is so popular

Tennis great, Steffi Graf

with both Germans and tourists. It started back in the fifteenth century. Today it is the biggest book fair in the world. Guests can choose from nearly 400,000 books from hundreds of different publishers. There are book readings and interviews with the authors.

Germans love to join clubs. One out of three Germans belongs to a sports club. Children might join sports clubs for soccer, volleyball, or basketball. In addition to sports clubs, adults enjoy music, crafts, and pet clubs. Whatever the interest, there is a German club for it. Germans take their clubs seriously and follow strict rules. The clubs are not expensive to join, since most of the staff are volunteers.

Germany has many castles that are hundreds of years old. They are popular

Neuschwanstein Castle

places to visit. Long ago, these castles were the homes of the rich and powerful. Along the Rhine River are the castles of the "robber barons." They made passing boats stop and pay a toll. The Neuschwanstein Castle, in the Bavarian Alps, was used as a model for Disney films and theme parks.

Displays made of Legos in Legoland

On weekends, German families enjoy their time together. They might take a trip into the countryside for a picnic or go for a hike in the mountains. For a real treat, a family might go to one of Germany's theme parks, such as Heidepark Soltau, Fantasialand, or Legoland. There are also funfairs that move from town to town. On Sundays, German families often take time for a traditional family meal of roast pork and noodles or dumplings.

In the summer, hiking in the southern mountains or in the many German forests is a favorite pastime. There are special paths or trails to follow, so hikers

Snowboarding is a popular sport.

will not get lost. In the winter, the same mountains are filled with people on skis, sleds, bobsleds, and ice skates.

Germany's central location makes it easy to travel to other nations. Many Germans spend their summer vacations exploring neighboring European countries. Others like to have a more exciting vacation, like a trip to the Australian outback or sailing in the Mediterranean Sea.

In-line Skating

The sport of in-line skating is becoming very popular with both children and adults. Sunday walks in the park have become Sunday skates in the park. All of Germany's large cities hold "blade nights" once a week. Streets are closed to regular traffic, and in-line skaters take them over. Late-night skating in some cities has become so popular that up to 30,000 skaters will come out. In Frankfurt, the police also *patrol* the streets on their skates.

Let's Celebrate!

In the small Bavarian town of Dinkelsbuhl, a ten-day Children's Festival called *Kinderzeche* (Children's Reckoning) is held each year in July. In 1632, during the Thirty Years' War, the Swedish army had surrounded Dinkelsbuhl and was

Dressed for the Children's Festival in Dinkelsbuhl

about to destroy it. A group of brave children, led by a young girl named Kinderlore, begged the Swedish general to spare them. The general felt so sorry for them that he and his soldiers left the town unharmed. Today, the children of Dinkelsbuhl dress in costumes from the 1600s and march through the streets. The whole town celebrates with a play, parades, brass bands, and dancing.

Most Germans celebrate Weihnachten (Christmas) on December 24 and 25. They exchange presents on Christmas Eve. Then, they go to church and eat a large feast on Christmas Day. Most people keep their Christmas trees up until the Epiphany, on January 6.

Frankfurt sparkles with holiday lights.

Santa trades his sleigh for a motorcycle.

In addition to Christmas, families in Germany also celebrate Nikolaustag (Saint Nicholas Day) on December 6. The night before, children put their shoes outside the door or out on a windowsill, hoping that Saint Nicholas will bring them a treat. They might find candy or presents inside their shoes in the morning.

Ostern, or Easter, is an important religious holiday. Holy Week includes Palm Sunday, Good Friday, and Easter Sunday. German children enjoy many of the same activities as American children, such as decorating eggs and going on Easter egg hunts. Plastic eggs are hung from outdoor trees. A donkey on wheels is often a part of Palm Sunday parades, remembering how Jesus entered Jerusalem. Since

Easter in Germany

palms do not grow in Germany, children take pussy willows or hazelnut twigs to church. In the Black Forest, tall poles are decorated and carried to church. Easter Sunday is spent going to church and after that, enjoying a midday meal with the family. Holy Week is also a time for spring cleaning.

Children in Germany celebrate their birthdays much like they do in the United States. They have friends over for a party with food and games. They are given presents. They blow out candles on the birthday cake and sing "Zum Gerburtstag viel Gluck," which means "good luck for your birthday."

Sometimes children play a game with chocolate at their birthday parties. A large piece of chocolate is put in the middle of the table. When a player throws the dice and gets a six, he puts on a silly hat and a pair of gloves and tries to eat the chocolate with a knife and fork. As soon as someone else gets a six, he must pass the clothes and chocolate to the next player. This continues until there is no chocolate left.

Germany's Octoberfest is known around the world. Millions of visitors come to Munich in Bavaria each year to enjoy Bavarian food, beer, and lively bands. Beer tents are put up around the city, each of which can hold up to 6,000 people. The celebration lasts for sixteen days.

Getting married in Germany can be hard work! Before they get married, a couple goes to a party called a *polterabend*. Guests smash dishes into pieces to scare away evil spirits. The couple must clean

Octoberfest in Munich

up the mess together as a test to see if they will get along in hard times. In south Germany, there is a tradition where newlyweds find a log outside the church. They must saw it in half while wearing their wedding clothes. And in the north, wedding guests play a trick on the bride and groom. They put all their furniture on the roof of their house, and watch the couple as they move it all back inside.

In the villages of Germany, it is a long-held tradition to hold a "Richtfest" when a house is half-built. After the house is completely framed out in wood, but before the walls of brick or plaster go up, the builder and the homeowner take time to party. People bring gifts and say good-bye to the carpenters, whose work is done. A green wreath is put on the roof for good luck.

The Day of German Unity on October 3 is Germany's newest holiday. After World War II, Germany was divided into two separate nations. A great wall was built between East and West Germany. The wall divided Berlin in half, with soldiers standing guard to make sure no one escaped from the East to the West. The Day of German Unity celebrates the time on October 3, 1990, when the divided Germany finally became one nation again.

A child holds the German flag.

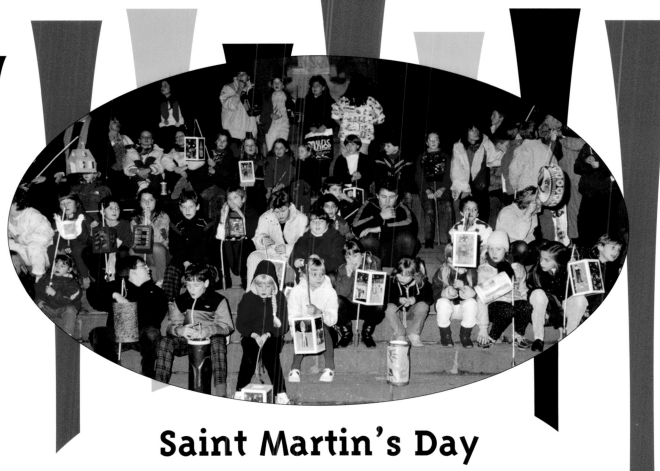

Saint Martin's Day

Saint Martin's Festival, or *Martinstag*, is one of the most popular of the saints' days in Germany. Saint Martin was a Roman soldier who lived in the fourth century. There is a legend that says he cut his coat in half to share it with a poor man who was about to die from the cold. His holiday is celebrated on November 11. On the night before, children carry lanterns through the streets and sing special songs. A man dressed as Saint Martin travels with them on horseback. Sometimes, the night ends with the adults and children building a bonfire. Children enjoy a *weckmann*, a sweet roll baked in the shape of a man with raisins for eyes and a white pipe in his mouth.

The German flag has three stripes: a black one on top, a red one in the middle, and a gold one on the bottom. It is supposed to mean "out of the darkness (black), through blood (red), and into the sunshine (gold)."

Germany is a member of the European Union, which uses the euro as its form of money. Euro coins share common European designs on the front, but the designs on the back of the coins change from nation to nation. Euro banknotes are the same in all the EU nations. As of April 2004, one euro was equal to $1.21 in the United States.

Count in German

English	German	Say it like this:
one	eins	eyns
two	zwei	tsvigh
three	drei	dry
four	vier	feer
five	fünf	fuenf
six	sechs	zeks
seven	sieben	ZEE-bin
eight	acht	akht
nine	neun	noin
ten	zehn	tsane

Glossary

autobahn   A German highway.

continent   One of the seven main areas of land on the earth.

heather   A low-growing plant that has tiny purple flowers.

objections   Reasons for not liking something.

patent   The government's agreement to let only one person make or sell something.

patrol   To make regular trips around something in order to guard or keep it safe.

printing press   A machine that prints words and pictures on paper.

restore   To put back into an earlier condition.

rivets   Metal fasteners that keep two pieces together.

whirlpool   Water that moves quickly in a circle, and pulls things toward the center.

Fast Facts

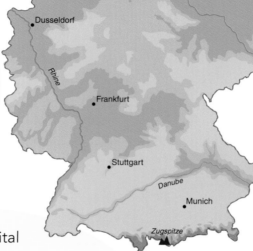

Germany's official name is the Federal Republic of Germany. The country is divided into sixteen provinces, or states. Each state can make its own laws.

Germany is the third-largest nation in the European Union after France and Spain. It also has the most people of any country in the EU. It is a little smaller than the state of Montana.

Berlin is the capital of Germany. During World War II, almost 90 percent of Berlin's buildings were destroyed. Today, new buildings are going up and old buildings are being restored.

The high snowy peaks of the German Bavarian Alps form the southern border with Austria and Switzerland. The tallest of these snowy peaks is Zugspitze, at 9,718 feet (2,962 m).

The German flag has three stripes: a black one on top, a red one in the middle, and a gold one on the bottom. It is supposed to mean "out of the darkness (black), through blood (red), and into the sunshine (gold)."

In Germany, 34 percent of the people are Protestant, 34 percent are Roman Catholic, 3.7 percent are Muslim, and 28.3 percent follow other religions.

Germany is a member of the European Union, which uses the euro as its form of money. As of April 2004, one euro was equal to $1.21 in the United States.

The Rhine River is an important river that runs from Switzerland through Germany and into the Netherlands. It is 820 miles (1,319 km) long and connects southern and northern Europe.

Germany was one of the first countries to build highways, in 1913. These highways are called the autobahn.

As of July 2004, there were 82,424,609 people living in Germany.

Germany's largest lake, the Bodensee, is in the south. It is called Lake Constance in English. Half of the Bodensee is in Germany, and the rest is in Switzerland and Austria.

Proud to Be German

Martin Luther (1483–1546)

Martin Luther was born on November 10, 1483, in Eiselben. He was a law student before becoming a Catholic monk and professor of theology at Wittenberg University. He began to complain against one of the church's practices. People were encouraged to buy pieces of paper, called indulgences, that said their sins were forgiven. Luther felt that this idea was not in the Bible, and he wanted to let the church leaders know his views. On the evening of October 31, 1517, he nailed his 95 Theses, or *objections*, to the door of Castle Church in Wittenberg. His views became very popular in Germany and spread quickly to other countries. Leaders in the Roman Catholic Church wanted him to change his mind, but he would not. Luther's movement to change the church became known as the Protestant Reformation, and his followers were called Lutherans. Martin Luther translated the Bible into the German language for the first time.

Levi Strauss (1829–1902)

Levi Strauss was born on February 26, 1829, in Bavaria. At the age of 16, he came to New York and worked as a tailor. In 1853, he moved to San Francisco during the

California gold rush. He opened a general store and hoped to make and sell tents and wagon covers to the miners. He was going to use a canvas material called "cotton duck." Instead, he used the material to make strong work pants for the miners. Strauss used copper *rivets* to make them stronger. In 1873, he took out a *patent* for his pants. The miners loved the pants and they were an immediate success. His company, Levi Strauss & Co., was worth six million dollars by the time Strauss died. Today, his famous blue jeans are worn all around the world.

Katarina Witt (1965–)

Katarina Witt was born on December 3, 1965, in Staaken, Germany. Her father was in charge of a factory and her mother was a physical therapist. Katarina began kindergarten at age five and on walks to school she would pass by the Kuchwald Ice Arena. She begged her mother to let her try this sport, and finally her mother said yes. Katarina's talent for ice-skating was obvious right from the start. She tried out for and was accepted to the sports school. When she was nine years old, Katarina was discovered by one of Germany's most successful coaches, Jutta Mueller. She won two Olympic Gold Medals in 1984 and 1988, and was the World Figure Skating Champion four times. In 1990, Katarina also won an Emmy Award for her role in *Carmen on Ice.*

Find Out More

Books

Countries of the World: Germany by Michael Dahl. Capstone Press, Minnesota, 1997.

Dropping in on Germany by Amy Allison. The Rourke Book Company, Florida, 2001.

Enchantment of the World: Germany by Jean F. Blashfield. Children's Press, Connecticut, 2003.

Germany: The People by Kathryn Lane. Crabtree Publishing Co., New York, 2001.

Nations of the World: Germany by Greg Nickles and Niki Walker. Raintree Steck-Vaughn Co., Texas, 2001.

Web Sites*

Connect to the German Embassy, the German Information Center, and the Consulates General at **www.germany-info.org**.

Learn about German culture, history, places to visit, major cities, and geographical regions at **www.about-germany.org**.

Video

Germany. Globe Trekker Video. VHS, 50 minutes. 2001.

*All Internet sites were available and accurate when sent to press.

Index

Page numbers for illustrations are in **boldface.**

About the Author

Sharon Gordon has written many nature and science books for young children. She has worked as an advertising copywriter and a book club editor. She is writing other books for the *Discovering Cultures* series. Sharon and her husband Bruce have three teenage children, Douglas, Katie, and Laura, and one spoiled pooch, Samantha. They live in Midland Park, New Jersey. The family especially enjoys traveling to the Outer Banks of North Carolina. After she puts her three children through college, Sharon hopes to visit the many exciting places she has come to love through her writing and research.